Aftermath of the Syria-Turkey Earthquake

Incidents that lead to the death of Christian atsu

John Snow

Table of contents

Chapter 1

Aftermath of the Earthquake

On February 6, 2023, an enormous 7.8 size tremor, trailed not very far behind by a 7.6 extent consequential convulsion struck Turkey, its focal point nearest to the city of Kahramanmaras. North of 50,000 individuals has kicked the bucket by and large because of building implodes, with setbacks extending from Turkey to adjoining Syria. Past the loss of life and annihilation, the tremor has likewise made more extensive natural worries, both prompt and long haul.

The seismic action seriously harmed the water and disinfection framework in the district. As associations like the World Wellbeing Association (WHO) and the US's Government Crisis The board Organization have recognized, disturbance to water administrations brought about by tremors expands the gamble of waterborne illnesses and episodes of transmittable illnesses, and survivors ought to be promptly helped with the area and arrangement of clean water. Turkish well-being specialists have had the option to offer lockjaw shots for the people who demand it, with the WHO offering extra help in observing waterborne illnesses. The Unified Countries is likewise giving a guide, including the appropriation of cholera tests. In any case, brief drinking water sources and sterile washing and bathroom offices have been excessively not many to help those affected, and fixing basic water foundations will stay a drawn-out issue. No structures in the urban communities stayed in salvageable shape, because of the huge size of the effect, with as numerous as 5.3 million individuals in Syria losing their homes and encountering uprooting. Around 3,000 individuals figured out how to track down brief convenience, with 380,000 looking for cover in schools and training offices. The locale had not confronted a significant seismic tremor in over 200 years and was tremendously caught off guard by the fiasco.

The greatest concern, in any case, is for northwestern Syria, where 12 years of contention has previously left 4 million individuals uprooted and vigorously dependent on help and philanthropic help. The seismic tremor harmed the Hatay air terminal in Syria, as well as Bab al-Hawa, the street used to move help at the line, which the Turkish government controls. This, among other harmed streets and foundations in Southern Turkey, has created critical setbacks for shipments and has slowed down help arriving at affected pieces of Syria. These deferrals have previously cost a large number of lives, with help unfit to arrive at survivors pulled out of the rubble, and an absence of assets for those uprooted and without fundamental necessities.

The tremor has additionally made land issues. The beachfront city of Iskenderun experienced subsidence, which thus prompted flooding in the region. Some seaside networks have even experienced infringement from ocean water similar to 200 meters inland. Notwithstanding the danger of waterborne infections depicted beforehand, numerous slopes are in danger of landslips, and satellite symbolism shows proof of various avalanches and rockfalls. The impact of the land issues could have extra effects on the foundation, with streets and pipelines waiting to be revamped and diverted, and provincial networks will probably be lopsidedly impacted in contrast with metropolitan networks.

The calamity in Kahramanmaras likewise asks a more profound inquiry: how do people make networks that can exist as one with the inborn difficulties that the climate presents? Specifically, numerous urban areas that exist in tremor-inclined networks should view incredibly the test of developing homes and structures made to endure huge seismic movement. After horrendous seismic tremors in 1999 and 2011, Turkish specialists fixed development guidelines to have more structures retrofitted for earthquakes. Turkish authorities have answered the various fallen structures in the latest shake by exploring north of 130 individuals associated with the development of those structures and in any event, confining a few project workers they accept to be to blame.

All things being equal, there is likewise proof that the actual guidelines were not severely authorized, which might put some piece of the fault back on the pieces of the Turkish government answerable for implementing them. There is no conspicuous response to the subject of the people's relationship with their current circumstance, yet regulation can be one device in overcoming difficulties, particularly where regulation or guidelines can be made or upheld to safeguard individuals, basic foundation, and the climate. The Turkey-Syria tremors highlight the indispensable significance of pursuing a response to that inquiry.

Days after two strong seismic tremors shook southern Turkey and northern Syria, in what has been portrayed as one of the deadliest of the 21st 100 years, the loss of life has outperformed 46,000. Many towns have been decreased to rubble with six-story structures disintegrating right away. Following five days, there was at that point a bad situation for the dead in the graveyards of the impacted locales while countless individuals were dozing outside, in frequently freezing conditions. Many have rested in their vehicles or stopgap tents as the market slows down, with no place else to go. For over seven days, heroes worked constantly, hampered by an enormous winter storm, trying to track down the survivors. Children, youngsters, and once in a while whole families were pulled, still alive, from the rubble to the praise of individuals and the tears of family members. Some made due for as long as 11 days covered underneath the remaining parts of their homes. That's what numerous families said, in the initial not many days after the tremors, they could make out the weak voices of family members under the flotsam and jetsam. Then, gradually, quietness fell over the heaps of cement and blocks that were once homes and are presently burial chambers.

For 60 hours, Barış Yapar attempted to recover his grandparents' bodies from under the rubble of their own home. With his folks, Habip and Sevcan, the 27-year-old clinical brain science understudy attempted to no end to eliminate them. It was frantic work. It required two entire days after the two tremors before Turkey's true debacle help organization arrived at the town of

Samandağ close to the Syrian line. At the point when they at long last showed up, the modest number of heroes was extended flimsy. The Yapars looked as salvage laborers pulled individuals from the crushed concrete, various whom they had known for ages. As in different spots impacted by the seismic tremor, the Samandağ burial ground had no more space for different bodies. The newly dug graves are set apart with clear tombstones, with just bits of torn material assembled from the casualties' clothing to recognize them.

 In the city outside the Nurdağı graveyard in the Turkish territory of Gaziantep, many bodies lie heaped on top of one another on a line of pickup trucks, ready to be covered. No less than five imams have raced to Nurdağı to direct an unending surge of mass burial services, at times for upwards of 10 casualties on the double. Authorities got conveyances of caskets from adjoining towns to the extent that Istanbul gave a last resting spot to the mind-boggling quantities of bodies showing up in the town. However, even today, a huge number of individuals have been left on the roads. Numerous families go through the night before the vestiges of their homes, for dread that they might be plundered, warming themselves around a fire lit with wood assembled from the remaining parts of their own homes. The quake has intensified tons of helpful emergencies in Idlib. These homes of individuals currently inside were uprooted once when the Syrian system had gone after their towns, constraining them to look for cover in Idlib. Most said they had shown up so late that they had been snoozing houses with exposed substantial walls and little else. Idlib had been a position after all other options have run out for thousands uprooted by over 10 years of war. Across the area, a few set up their shelters among old Byzantine remains in sheer urgency for someplace to reside. The schools in Idlib, which had been changed over into emergency clinics, are imploding, where a couple of accessible specialists are in the middle of treating patients with intense wounds. These improvised offices are run on a tight budget and need the majority of the essential clinical supplies and prescriptions that are expected to treat quake survivors. Many youngsters were stranded after the seismic tremor, joining many vagrants from the conflict.

Turkey's administration has vowed to remake homes soon. Be that as it may, there's no such assistance (and considerably less other help) across the line in northwest Syria, where the tremor killed more than 4,500 individuals, harmed 8,500, destroyed around 10,000 structures, and left nearly 11,000 individuals destitute. Northwest Syria's occupants have no bound together government. They're caught in a conflict, a tradition of a 2011 unrest — some portion of the Bedouin Spring — that was smothered by the public authority of President Bashar al-Assad in a tactical activity supported by Russia. The locale is additionally really disconnected; there are just three (transitory) crossing directions for provisions toward contact with individuals along Syria's 900-kilometer line with Turkey.

Indeed, even before the tremors, the UN Office for the Coordination of Compassionate Issues assessed that the greater part of northwest Syria's 4.7 million individuals are inside uprooted, and around 70% of those are living in transitory convenience (frequently in rose urban communities). Multiple million need more to eat and 33% are handicapped, numerous on account of the conflict. Medical care offices have been designated, leaving just 66 clinics working, however inadequately prepared, during a continuous cholera flare-up.

The tremor has annihilated numerous Turkish and Syrian lives, homes, and jobs. The flood of help for salvage and recuperation endeavors has been amazing and soon both public and global partners will go to recreation. Carrying out the Türkiye Reduced isn't without its difficulties, yet an open door exists to make it part of plans to modify the district. Pushing ahead, it will be significant for Canada, the EU, and the US, in a joint effort with global offices, to begin investigating the minimized reception. The strategy wouldn't just basically support the local economy yet, in addition, assist with working on evacuees' confidence and host networks' flexibility. This wouldn't just add to a more noteworthy social union yet additionally diminish the probability of displaced persons optional developments and the need to raise assets for helpful help. At long last, it would comprise a substantial illustration of how the weight sharing portrayed in the

Worldwide Smaller on Evacuees can be executed extraordinarily and helpfully.

Chapter 2

Christian atsu's cause of death and his biography

Christian Atsu kicked his keep-going objective on February 5. He approached the soccer ball and pummeled it with his left foot, shooting it past 10 rival players and a goalie in the fifth moment of additional time. The ball tracked down the rear of the net, breaking a 0-0 tie and lifting his group to euphoric triumph. Atsu was quite far from the soil and rock pitches where he figured out how to play shoeless in Ghana. Be that as it may, through every one of the progressions — from neediness to proficient soccer, global popularity playing for Ghana, the ups and downs of the English Chief Association, and afterward another test with this group in Antakya, Turkey — he clung tightly to his confidence.

The Ghana global forward who played for Head Association clubs Chelsea and Newcastle lost his life in the tremor that hit Turkey. He was 31. Atsu played for the Turkish club Hatayspor in the Hatay area, which was hit hard by the tremor. Search groups recuperated Atsu's body in the remains of an extravagance 12-story building where he had been residing in the city of Antakya, Hatay territory, his chief said Saturday. A day after the seismic tremor there were reports that Atsu had been protected yet Hatayspor, after at first declaring that it had gotten data that Atsu was alive and en route to the clinic, said later that the reports of an effective salvage were mixed up and that he was all the while missing. It had likewise said the club's donning chief, Taner Savut, was all the while missing. Savut has not yet been found.

The project worker of the 12-story Ronesans Rezidans building — where Atsu and Savut resided — was kept at Istanbul Air terminal seven days prior, clearly attempting to leave the country. Atsu's representative, Nana Sechere, went to Turkey with Atsu's relatives trying to find him, clutching trust that he may be alive in the midst of the destruction. Sechere had asked specialists and Hatayspor authorities to increase their determination in the quest for Atsu and Savut. In an explanation Tuesday, Sechere said heroes had the option to pinpoint Atsu's definite room area in his fell high rise north of seven days after the overwhelming tremor yet the main thing they recuperated were two sets of his shoes.

Atsu played more than multiple times for Ghana and scored on his presentation as a 20-year-old in 2012. He was important for the Ghana crew at the 2014 World Cup in Brazil and featured at the 2015 African Cup of Countries, scoring two objectives to help Ghana to the last, where it lost in a punishment shootout to Ivory Coast. He was named the player of the competition at the

African Cup. Atsu was endorsed by Chelsea in 2013 yet his time there was restricted to appearances in show games and he was conveyed borrowed to different clubs for the following four years. The winger joined Newcastle borrowed in 2016 and was essential for the group that won advancement back to the Head Association in the 2016-17 season. Christian Atsu was dedicated to Christianity. In interviews, he has been straightforward about his strict convictions and has said that they have kept him grounded and centered all through his profession. Atsu has likewise taken part in various causes and charitable exercises, like giving cash to help the development of schools and the arrangement of clean water in his local Ghana.

Christian Atsu's initial encounters, identity, ethnicity, and religion all fundamentally impacted how he fostered his character and values personally and football player. He fills in as a motivation for hopeful youthful competitors in Ghana and all around the world because of his ability and steadiness. Christian Atsu and his twin sister, Christiana, were brought into the world by Immanuel and Afiko Twasam in Ada Foah on January 10, 1992. Immanuel was an unfortunate angler who battled to get enough fish in the mouth of the Volta Stream to accommodate his and Afiko's 10 youngsters. The family's circumstances developed direr when Immanuel kicked the bucket in 2004.

At 12 years of age, Atsu faulted himself for his dad's passing. If he had been working and bringing in cash as opposed to learning at a soccer foundation, he said, maybe the family might have paid for clinical medicines. His dad's last charge to him, nonetheless, was to adore God and consistently utilize his gifts to better humankind. The most ideal way he knew to do that was to continue to play soccer. Five years after his dad kicked the bucket, Atsu passed on Ghana to play proficient soccer for FC Porto — the top soccer group in Portugal. He remained on the seat however at that point was credited out to Rio Ave in 2011, where he scored without precedent for an expert game at age 17 and was named the group's player of the year.

Atsu attempted to conform to Portugal yet he met and went gaga for his significant other, and his playing improved quickly. In 2012, he began playing for Ghana's public group, acquiring acknowledgment from the global soccer press. The next year, he endorsed Chelsea and moved to the UK to play in the Chief Association. The West London club chose not to put him on the pitch, however, and on second thought credited him out to a progression of lower-association groups. In 2016, Atsu moved from Chelsea to Newcastle, marking a four-year contract for a detailed £6.2 million (about $8.4 million). At the point when the then 24-year-old soccer star moved to Newcastle, he and his family began going to the neighborhood Hillsong. The congregation was at that point went to by a few expert soccer players and known, locally, for running a games program for evacuee kids. There were various African foreigners in the assemblage, including a more seasoned couple from Ghana who welcomed Atsu like family.

Supported by the congregation and the memory of his dad's charge to better mankind, Atsu began working with Arms around the kid in 2017. He filled in as a diplomat for the charity and fund-raised to assist them with building a school for vagrants in Ghana. His endeavors subsidized the acquisition of land and an establishment in 2019, and he and by supporting a large part of the development. Presently, the school is close to the end, as indicated by Arms Around the Kid, yet at the same time needs paint and school supplies. Fans are arranging to complete the work.

Atsu likewise provided to help kids who had been compelled to work get the opportunity to return to school, and he discreetly contributed assets to the CrimeCheck Establishment to let individuals out of jail. In 2019, he paid a large number of pounds to deliver a 62-year-elderly person carrying out a punishment for taking under $2 worth of grain to take care of her loved ones. At the point when his generosity pulled in press consideration, English columnists proposed he was liberal on account of his involvement in destitution. Atsu revised them. It wasn't so much that, he said. He was roused by his confidence.

Atsu is made due by his sister, spouse, two children, and a girl.

Chapter 3

Will there be another Earthquake?

The high loss of life from the huge tremor in southeastern Turkey and northern Syria is by and large a consequence of the poor underlying uprightness of thousands of structures, specialists say.

For this reason, Istanbul, a city of 15 million individuals which geologists anticipate will ultimately get hit by serious areas of strength for a, could see a huge number of passings except if a move is made on a great many structures in the city that aren't quake-proof or safe. While endeavors have been made to modernize building regulations and safeguard against quakes, specialists say there is a tremendous test progressing in years to structures sufficiently safe to endure a tremor.

More than 17,000 individuals have been killed by the 7.8-size quake that hit recently around 26 km east of the Turkish city of Nurdagi at a profundity of around 18 km on the East Anatolian Shortcoming. Turkey lies on two significant shortcoming frameworks, the North Anatolian Issue and East Anatolian Issue, making it the country around there with the most elevated hazard to be impacted by a shudder. Seismic tremor scientists foresee that a quake of extent 7.0 or more grounded is probably going to strike Istanbul, which is near the North Anatolian Shortcoming, in the following 70 years.

Gauges differ as to possible misfortunes of life if a tremor struck Istanbul. The region of Istanbul led its review assessing that 14,500 individuals will bite the dust assuming that a size 7.5 seismic tremor occurs around evening time. One concentrate by a gathering of European scientists projected 30,000 to 40,000 would be dispensed with.

Be that as it may, Bal accepts those evaluations are low, with his review assessing 47,000 structures would be obliterated, with the chance of 150,000 individuals killed. The issues in Istanbul are the very issues that have become known in this latest seismic tremor — a large number of the structures in Turkey have all the earmarks of being very powerless.

Just from her underlying perceptions of the harm, Faure Walker said the annihilated structures she finds in pictures and video appear to come up short on tremor-safe designs, such as built-up cement or section propping. The shortcoming framework that caused the current week's staggering size of 7.8 seismic tremors and 7.5 extents delayed repercussion in Turkey has recently set off different shudders that have impacted a wide area of the Center East.

It's difficult to anticipate future tremor successions; pinpointing the specific overall setting of destroying shakes in front of when they hit is the stuff of sci-fi. However, a basic guideline of likelihood is that enormous quakes can sire different seismic tremors. Along the shortcoming framework that burst in Monday's earthquakes in Turkey, a shake almost quite a while back was consequently trailed by a grouping of tremors toward the south.

The Turkey quake happened on the East Anatolian shortcoming framework, which begins the eastern finish of the North Anatolian issue and stretches out toward the southwest, around the Syrian line. In the end, the framework broadens toward the south and turns into the Dead Ocean Change issue framework, going through beachfront Syria, Lebanon, Israel, and Jordan to the Red Ocean. Dolan expressed that a portion of the seismic burdens from Monday's shudders in Turkey have been sent toward the northern finish of the Dead Ocean Change issue framework.

Around a long time back, there was a progression of huge extent seismic tremors that spread from the East Anatolian issue, from north to south. The tremors burst the shortcoming in a similar region hit Monday. Throughout the long term, there were about six strong quakes, moving toward the south on the issue framework through beachfront Syria into Lebanon, at last finishing in an exceptionally enormous tremor on the Dead Ocean Change shortcoming framework in 1202, essentially focused in Lebanon however broadening farther south.

As of not long ago, the East Anatolian issue has drawn less consideration than the North Anatolian shortcoming, which stumbles into northern Turkey, from east to west. The North Anatolian shortcoming is perilously near the country's most crowded city of Istanbul. In the mid-twentieth hundred years, a progression of enormous tremors started breaking along the North Anatolian shortcoming, beginning with the staggering greatness 7.8 Erzincan quake in 1939 that caused an expected 32,700 passings.

The latest huge shakes in that arrangement were the extent 7.6 Izmit tremors of August 1999, which struck east of Istanbul and brought about an expected 17,000 passings. It was followed three months after the fact by the extent 7.2 Duzce tremor, which struck farther east. One part of the North Anatolian shortcoming that hasn't yet burst from that point forward runs near Istanbul.

The East Anatolian issue framework has drawn in lesser consideration, to some degree since it hasn't produced pulverizing seismic tremors as the North Anatolian did in the twentieth hundred years. The North Anatolian has generally been viewed as a significant danger: Its developed shortcoming framework is smooth, long, and straight, which clarifies its capacity for producing super shakes as extensive as extent 7.8.

Turkey has been hit by a few tremors previously and there is a high likelihood that they will be hit with another soon however knowing precisely when that would be is a reality that hasn't been known at this point.